WEEKLY READER BOOKS PRESENTS

Bicycles Are Fun to Ride

By Dorothy Chlad

Illustrations by Lydia Halverson

WEEKLY READER BOOKS
Middletown, Connecticut

Note: Bicycles are shown without reflectors because young riders should not ride their bicycles at night.

Weekly Reader Books offers several exciting card and activity programs. For information, write to WEEKLY READER BOOKS, P.O. Box 16636, Columbus, Ohio 43216.

This book is a presentation of Weekly Reader Books. Weekly Reader Books offers book clubs for children from preschool through high school.

For further information write to:
WEEKLY READER BOOKS
4343 Equity Drive
Columbus, Ohio 43228

Library of Congress Cataloging in Publication Data

Chlad, Dorothy.
    Bicycles are fun to ride.

    (Safety Town)
    Summary: A young boy tells how he enjoys riding his bicycle while remembering important safety rules.
    1. Cycling—Juvenile literature. 2. Bicycles—Safety measures—Juvenile literature. 3. Cycling—Safety measures—Juvenile literature. [1. Bicycles and bicycling—Safety measures. 2. Safety] I. Halverson, Lydia, ill. II. Title. III. Series: Chlad, Dorothy. Safety Town.
GV1043.5.C45   1984   796.6'0289   83-23234
ISBN O-516-O1975-9   AACR2

Hi, my name is Mark.

This is my bicycle.

Mom and dad gave it to me for my birthday.

Seat

Handle Bars

Spoke

Chain

Pedal

Chain Guard

Tire

They showed me
all the parts of the
bicycle.

Before I ride my bicycle, I check the parts.

Sometimes my sister
helps me.

If any parts are loose
or broken, we fix them.

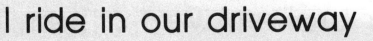

I ride in our driveway

and on the sidewalk.

I am careful when
people are walking.

Before my sister and
I cross the street, I look
left—right—left.

I live on a busy
street. There are a lot of
cars, trucks, buses, and
motorcycles. I cannot
ride in the street.

My friends live in the
country. They must be
very careful.

I have a lot of fun
riding my bicycle. I
ride to the playground,
to my friend's house,
and to the library.

Sometimes my
friends and I ride to
the park to watch our
brothers and sisters
play.

On special days, we decorate our bikes.

Then we ride in the
parade.

When I finish riding, I _ALWAYS_ put my bicycle away. I put it in a safe place so it does not get broken.

You can have a lot
of fun too, if you
remember my bicycle
safety rules:

1. Ride where mom and dad tell you.

2. Check your bicycle parts.

3. Fix loose or broken parts.

4. Put your bicycle in a safe place.

5. *Always* be careful.

About the Author

Dorothy Chlad, founder of the total concept of Safety Town, is recognized internationally as a leader in Preschool/Early Childhood Safety Education. She has authored eight books on the program, and has conducted the only workshops dedicated to the concept. Under Mrs. Chlad's direction, the National Safety Town Center was founded to promote the program through community involvement.

She has presented the importance of safety education at local, state, and national safety and education conferences, such as National Community Education Association, National Safety Council, and the American Driver and Traffic Safety Education Association. She serves as a member of several national committees, such as the Highway Traffic Safety Division and the Educational Resources Division of National Safety Council. Chlad was an active participant at the Sixth International Conference on Safety Education.

Dorothy Chlad continues to serve as a consultant for State Departments of Safety and Education. She has also consulted for the TV program, "Sesame Street" and recently wrote this series of safety books for Childrens Press.

A participant of White House Conferences on safety, Dorothy Chlad has received numerous honors and awards including National Volunteer Activist and YMCA Career Woman of Achievement. In 1983, Dorothy Chlad was one of sixty people nationally to receive the **President's Volunteer Action Award** from President Reagan for twenty years of Safety Town efforts.

About the Artist

Lydia Halverson was born Lydia Geretti in midtown Manhattan. When she was two, her parents left New York and moved to Italy. Four years later her family returned to the United States and settled in the Chicago Area. Lydia attended the University of Illinois, graduating with a degree in fine arts. She worked as a graphic designer for many years before finally concentrating on book illustration.

Lydia lives with her husband and two cats in a suburb of Chicago and is active in several environmental organizations.

DATE DUE

#47-0108 Peel Off Pressure Sensitive